Character Education,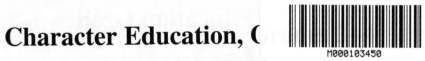

Character Education Grades 3–4
Introduction

Character is the inner nature of a person. It determines how a person thinks, feels, and acts. Given the fundamental importance of character, it is vital that we teach our children the values that will enable them to make decisions that better themselves, their community, and the world.

This program is designed to assist you in developing these positive character traits. The six basic traits targeted in *Character Education* are: caring, fairness, trustworthiness, responsibility, respect, and citizenship. The teaching of these traits follows the standards established by the Character Education Partnership (CEP). The stories and activities can be integrated into the curriculum as a supplemental source that promotes a strong character foundation as prescribed by the Partnerships in Character Education Pilot Project.

Organization

There are seven units, six based on one of the core character traits. The last unit is a wrap-up unit that covers all six traits. Each unit focuses on a story that exhibits the trait or traits. Follow-up activities develop understanding and provide a context for application. The units incorporate the following elements:

Teacher Information: This page defines the core character trait and lists the qualities of that trait in language that students can understand. It also summarizes the story and briefly offers suggestions for introducing the activity pages. Finally, the page outlines a group project to be completed over the course of study as well as a list of books to further support the teaching of the character trait.

Story: The story selections introduce the character trait and serve as a model. The selections are high interest and on grade level. They provide an excellent point of departure for discussion, especially through the "Think and Talk" question at the end of each story.

Moreover, they represent a variety of genres for easy integration into a language arts curriculum.

Story Response: The story response page has five questions. The first two are comprehension questions that relate directly to the story. The third and fourth questions ask students to reflect on the character trait. The last question asks students how they demonstrate that character trait in their daily life.

Activities: The follow-up activities focus on the basic qualities that make up each trait. These activities are fun, interesting, and varied enough to engage students, thereby increasing participation and learning. Many activities are open-ended in order to challenge all learners and encourage success.

The first activity following the story response is to be used in conjunction with the theme bulletin board. It asks students to notice when their classmates exhibit one of the targeted traits, such as fairness, caring, or respect. Using the cutouts that correspond to each trait, students write the name of the classmates who demonstrated good character as well as a brief summary of what they observed. The students then hang the cutouts on the theme bulletin board.

The remaining activities can be used in multiple curriculum areas. Some encourage writing, making charts, drawing, or playing a game.

Use

To begin, determine the implementation that best fits your students' needs and your classroom structure. The following plan suggests a format for this implementation:

In advance, prepare a classroom bulletin board that displays the character symbol and lists the qualities. You may also wish to photocopy the blackline masters on the back of the pull-out activity cards to pass out to students.

1. Introduce the core character trait. Lead a discussion of the character symbol and how it represents the trait.

2. Read the story. Follow each story with a class discussion identifying how the story represents the trait. Encourage students to share what they learn from the story.

3. Complete the story response.

4. Pass out the first activity related to the bulletin board. Explain that students should look for examples of the targeted trait during the course of the unit. When the unit is complete, remove the cutouts from the bulletin board and pass them out to the students whose names are on them. You may wish to provide a treat for anyone whose name is shown.

5. Remaining activities can be implemented as time permits.

Additional Notes

Character Symbol: Each character trait is represented with a graphic tree symbol to serve as a visual cue and reminder. These symbols appear on the corresponding unit pages, activity card posters, blackline masters, and awards.

Parent Letter: Send the Letter to Parents home with students.

Interview: During each unit, have students choose a person who they think exemplifies the character trait. Have students use the form on page 58 to interview that person.

Self-Assessment: Students can use page 59 to tell when they have demonstrated good character. You may wish to ask them to complete a form daily, weekly, or over the course of the unit.

Calendar: The calendar on page 60 can be used for a wide range of unit activities, such as recording good character behavior or logging assignments in order to encourage responsible work habits.

Awards: Individual character awards can be found on pages 61–63. You may wish to make copies of them and give them to students to recognize and reinforce good character behavior.

Activity Card Posters: Four-color posters showing the character symbols can be found in the back of the book. It is highly recommended that you display on a bulletin board the poster showing the symbol, as several activities are related to it.

Blackline Masters: Blackline masters showing the symbol and listing each quality can be found on the back of the activity card posters. You may wish to make copies for students to color and take home during the unit.

These blackline masters can also be used as covers for individual, group, or class books. Each child or group contributes writing or art about character. Then, the pages are assembled into book form, with the blackline masters as the covers.

Dominoes: Cut out the individual domino pieces for students to play in an activity center. Up to three players begin with five dominoes. They should match words to a symbol. Other uses might include: students draw a domino to determine the group they will work in; students draw a domino and identify one quality associated with the word or symbol; students play concentration, forming word or picture pairs.

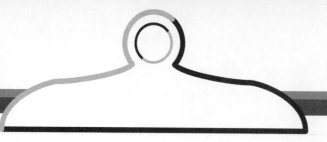

Dear Parent,

As parents and teachers, we try to teach our children basic manners and values in order to help them become respected and productive members of the family and community. These values emphasize the character traits we wish to impart to our children. A strong character based on ethical values can help children make the right choices when faced with difficult situations. With the events of the past years, it is even more important that we work together to prepare our children to take their places in an increasingly complex world. If we prepare them adequately, our children will be able to make decisions that benefit themselves, their community, and the world.

During the year, your child will learn about the six core traits of character: caring, fairness, trustworthiness, respect, responsibility, and citizenship. From time to time, I may send home activity pages. Some of these may have been completed in class, while others are to be completed at home. To reinforce the importance of character growth and development, please consider the following suggestions:

- Together, go over the completed work your child brings home.

- For assignments that are to be completed at home, provide your child a place to work, and then review the work when it is finished.

- Encourage your child to explain the basic qualities of the character trait being studied.

- Point out ways your child, family members, or community members exhibit the qualities.

- Offer praise when your child shows the character trait.

- Inquire about the progress of the group project.
  (You might even like to help!)

Thank you for your help. Your child and I appreciate your assistance and reinforcement in this learning process.

Cordially,

Caring

Caring is one of the basic traits of character. It is the true and honest concern for others. Most people are genuine in their spirit of love and giving. However, some caring can be a disguise for giving with the expectation of getting something in return. Stress to students the difference in giving to get something in return and giving because it makes others—and the giver—feel good.

The basic qualities of caring include:
- Help and comfort those in need.
- Be kind and considerate to all.
- Thank those who do a kindness.
- Forgive those who are mean or thoughtless.
- Give to others in time and money—charity—to make their life better.

About the Symbol

For students, the most obvious way to show caring is to help and comfort those in need. In many cultures, food is given to others in times of joy and sorrow. The basket of apples represents providing food when someone is busy or ill, showing that someone took extra time and thought to care for another person.

About the Story (pages 6–9)

The Weaver and the Princess: A Malaysian Folktale retold by Kir Dan
On the way to the palace to ask to marry the Princess Poh, a kind but poor weaver stops people from hurting some animals. The animals return to help the weaver as he faces challenges to win the hand of the princess.

About the Activities

Activity 1: Caring Apples (page 10)
If possible, provide an apple snack for the class. Lead students in a discussion of how the apple can be a symbol for caring. Encourage them to be creative in their responses. Next, remind students to use the apples to recognize when classmates show caring behavior throughout the unit. You may wish to provide a special treat for students whose names appear on the tree.

Activity 2: A Caring Letter (page 11)
Discuss with students the qualities of caring exhibited in *The Weaver and the Princess*. Then explain that caring also involves showing and expressing thanks when someone shows kindness.

Activity 3: Caring Words (page 12)
Explain to students that emotions are the ways people feel. Review different emotions the characters in the story may have felt. Then brainstorm different emotions students feel and the situations in which they occur. Ask students to role-play what a caring person would do in each situation.

Group Project

Discuss with students the idea of charity—using time and money to help community members. Then brainstorm a list of community groups that might need help, such as a senior citizens' home or a food bank. Guide students to choose, plan, and complete a project to help one of the groups.

At-home

Ask students to find ways that family members show caring to each other.

Related Reading

The Giving Tree by Shel Silverstein
The Crane Wife by Odds Bodkin
Who's Sick Today? by Lynne Cherry

The Weaver and the Princess
A Malaysian Folktale
retold by Kir Dan

CARING

Once, long ago, there lived a kind, young weaver named Serungal (Ser•an•gôl). He wanted to marry Princess Poh (Pō). They had met in the town square and had talked for hours. Later Serungal couldn't get the gentle, clever woman out of his mind.

"But the king would want her to marry a rich man," Serungal said sadly.

Serungal was not rich, but he was a good weaver. For months he collected tiny bits of silk thread. When he had enough, Serungal decided to weave a fine cloth— fit for a princess.

When the silk cloth was finished, Serungal packed it in a bag. He set off to see the king.

"Perhaps the king will think the cloth is very fine. Then he will let me marry Princess Poh," he said.

On the road, Serungal saw a man. The man was about to squash an ant with his big sandal.

"Stop!" yelled Serungal. "Leave that ant alone. It has done nothing to hurt you. You have no reason to harm it."

The man looked up in surprise. The ant ran away. Serungal walked on.

Farther down the road, Serungal saw a boy throw a stone at a squirrel.

"Stop!" said Serungal. "That squirrel has done nothing to hurt you. You have no reason to harm it."

Surprised, the boy looked at Serungal. The squirrel hurried into the woods. Serungal walked on.

Sunset came. Serungal kept walking. As darkness fell, he heard people shouting.

"Get it!" said one man.

"Oh, no! I just missed it," said another.

Serungal saw they were trying to kill a firefly.

"Stop!" yelled Serungal. "That firefly has done nothing to hurt you. You have no reason to harm it."

The people looked up in surprise. The firefly flew away. Serungal walked on through the night.

The next morning, Serungal reached the palace. He showed the fine cloth to the guards at the gate. The guards were dazzled. They led Serungal right to the king.

"What do you want?" asked the king.

"I want to marry Poh, your daughter," explained Serungal.

He showed the king his cloth. The king was not happy. The cloth *was* very fine, but he wanted a rich son-in-law. The king thought for a minute.

Then he said, "If Poh agrees, you may marry her. But first you must do something. My guards will scatter a basket of rice in the woods. You will have four hours to pick up every grain."

Serungal watched the guards scatter the rice.

"It is impossible," cried Serungal. "I will never pick up all the rice in time."

"Don't worry," said a voice. Serungal looked down. He saw the ant he had saved. "I will help you. After all, you saved my life."

The ant called all his friends. They picked up every grain of rice. Within two hours, Serungal returned to the king with the basket full of rice.

The king was amazed. But he didn't show his surprise.

"If Poh agrees," said the king, "you may marry her. But first you must do something else. You must climb my nut tree and pick every nut," explained the king.

Serungal looked up the tree. He had never seen such a tall tree.

"It's impossible," said Serungal. "No one could climb to the top of that tree."

"Don't worry," said a voice. Serungal looked up. He saw the squirrel he had saved. "I will help you. After all, you saved my life."

The squirrel dashed to the top of the tree. It was easy for him to pick the nuts. Soon, Serungal returned to the palace with all the nuts.

The king was surprised. But he just said, "If Poh agrees, you may marry her. But you must do one more thing. I will send my seven daughters into a room with no light. They will say nothing. You must walk right to Poh."

The seven princesses went into the room. Then Serungal walked into the darkness. He couldn't see or hear anything.

"How will I ever find Poh?" he asked.

"Do not worry," a voice said. It was the firefly Serungal had saved. "I will help you. After all, you saved my life."

The firefly flew over the seven princesses, lighting up their faces. Serungal clearly saw Princess Poh.

The king was amazed. Serungal had done all he had asked.

"If Poh agrees, you may marry her," said the king.

Of course, Princess Poh agreed to marry Serungal right away. At their wedding, the princess wore the fine silk cloth Serungal had made. And they lived for many, many years together in the palace.

Think and Talk

What is caring? How did Serungal show caring?

Name _____ Date _____

Story Response

Directions

Answer the questions.

1. How does Serungal help the squirrel?

_____

_____

2. How do the ants help Serungal?

_____

_____

3. People show caring by helping. What are some other ways people show caring?

_____

_____

4. A caring person forgives others. How do people show they forgive each other?

_____

_____

5. What are some ways that you show caring in school?

_____

_____

_____

Name _____   Date _____

Caring Apples

CARING

One way to show caring is to be kind and considerate.

Directions

Look for ways your classmates show caring. On an apple, write the name of the classmate and tell how he or she showed caring. Then, hang the apple on the tree.

Name _____   Date _____

A Caring Letter

CARING

One way to show caring is to thank someone for his or her help.

Directions

Pretend to be one of the animals in the story. Write a letter to Serungal thanking him for saving your life.

_____

_____

_____

_____

_____

_____

_____

_____

_____

_____

_____

_____

_____

_____

_____

_____

_____

_____

_____

Name _____   Date _____

Caring Words

CARING

Emotions are the way people feel. People can be happy, sad, scared, angry, lonely, or surprised. A caring person will try to help someone who is not happy.

Directions

Look at each picture. Name the emotion. What could you say or do to help?

1.

_____

_____

_____

_____

_____

2.

_____

_____

_____

_____

_____

3.

_____

_____

_____

_____

_____

Fairness

Fairness is the character trait that values equality, impartiality in making decisions, and willingness to correct mistakes quickly. It can be a difficult concept for young people to understand at times; however, even young children can learn the importance of treating people equally.

The basic qualities of fairness include:
- Take turns and share.
- Treat people equally.
- Be open-minded and listen.
- Do not blame people carelessly.
- Do not take advantage of people.
- Let consequences fit the wrongful act.

About the Symbol

Many heated discussions take place at school where children are developing group-involvement skills. The playground is one place that is especially difficult, because there is little structure or guidance. Moreover, the swing, in particular, is the scene of unfair play and hurt feelings since the students who first get the equipment usually keep it for as long as they can. The tree with the two balanced swings serves as a reminder that fairness means treating people equally, sharing, and keeping an open mind.

About the Story (pages 14–17)

The Together Team by Janet Craig
Rosie, a good student, and Sarah, a good soccer player, prejudge each other. They learn about prejudice and how to overcome it when they have to complete a history assignment together.

About the Activities

Activity 1: A Fair Swing (page 18)
Invite volunteers to share playground situations in which they felt they were treated unfairly. Ask those students what would have made the situation fair. Then invite students to speculate why the swing is the symbol for the characteristic of fairness. Remind the class to look for ways that their classmates show fairness in the classroom *and* on the playground throughout the unit. You may wish to provide a small treat for students whose names appear on the tree.

Activity 2: Fair or Foul? (page 19)
Lead students in a discussion of good sportsmanship. Invite them to share why being fair is part of being a good sport. Then introduce the concept of compromise.

Activity 3: Fair Square (page 20)
Review the qualities of fairness and invite students to give an example of each.

Group Project

Divide students into six groups. Assign each group one of the qualities of fairness listed above. Encourage them to think of how the value pertains to a school situation. Then have the group create a poster that represents the value. Allow students to hang the posters in the school hallways.

At-home

Ask students to draw a picture of a conflict they had with a brother or sister. Encourage them to bring the picture to school and tell how the situation was resolved.

Related Reading

One Fine Day by Nonny Hogrogian
The Great Gilly Hopkins by Katherine Paterson
Ramona Forever by Beverly Cleary

The Together Team
by Janet Craig

I honestly don't know how I let myself get talked into things. Take joining the soccer team. We had just moved to town. Mom and Dad thought joining a team was a great idea.

They said, "Give it a try, Rosie. You'll meet some new friends."

Finally, I said okay. But I didn't really feel okay about it. Sure, I like to kick a soccer ball around with a friend. But I wasn't too sure I wanted to be on a team.

I was even less sure when I showed up for practice. Those kids were good! A lot better than I was. I didn't know any of the players. And I didn't know the plays they had already worked out.

Finally, the ball came my way. I got ready to boot it. With all my might, I kicked—and missed it! I fell on my backside. Talk about humiliations!

Then I saw one of the kids looking at me. There was a grin on her face. Boy, was I mad! Who did she think she was?

I didn't play very hard after that. But I did notice that the girl who laughed at me was a great player. She could dribble the ball, pass it, and kick it exactly where she wanted to. Her name was Sarah.

When I got home that afternoon, Mom asked, "How was practice?"

"I was completely disgraced!" I said. "And I don't think the other kids liked me. I felt real hostility from them."

"Give them a chance," Mom said. "And give yourself a chance, too." It was her usual answer.

I had history homework to do. So I got busy. We were studying about segregation and how people had worked for equal rights. It was pretty interesting. I wasn't a soccer star, but I was a good student.

The next day our teacher, Mr. Montano, announced, "We're going to be doing some hands-on projects for our unit on equal rights. I'll be assigning 'study buddies.' Together, you'll come up with your own ideas about *prejudice*—and ways of fighting it."

He called out the names of the people who would be working together. My heart sank when I heard my name. "Rosie Acosta, you'll work with Sarah Jonsen."

Sarah Jonsen! The girl on the soccer team who had laughed at me! When I looked at her, she didn't look very happy. Well, neither was I.

The next afternoon, I headed for the library to study. I had just opened my books when I felt someone behind me. It was Sarah.

"I guess we should start our history project," I said.

"I guess so," said Sarah. She didn't sound as if she meant it.

"Well," I said, "I don't care if you don't want to work with me. I'm not going to let it ruin my project."

Sarah laughed. "You don't have to worry about that," she said. "You're a brain!"

I let that pass. We started to read the chapter.

"Look at the part where it talks about prejudice," I said. I waited. Sarah wasn't moving. Then I looked at her. She had tears in her eyes.

"I can't find it," she said. "I can't read as fast as you can."

Suddenly, I understood why Sarah hadn't wanted to work with me. "It's okay," I said.

We took our time reading the chapter. Soon we began to talk about *prejudice*. I said, "I thought you didn't like me because I can't play as well as you can."

"And I thought you didn't like me because I'm not a great student," she said.

"I guess we were both wrong," I said.

She nodded. "We should get to know somebody before we judge them." Then she said, "Hey, I know what we can do for our project— I'll teach you the plays for soccer. You'll be part of the team in no time. That's a way to fight prejudice, isn't it?"

"Right," I said. "I'll do it—but only if you promise to meet so that we can study together."

That's exactly what we did. It wasn't always easy, but we worked at it. I know Sarah was happy with the *A* she got on the history test.

Teaching me soccer was another story. She showed me how to dribble and pass the ball. And she asked the other kids to include me.

Our team was pretty good! We even made it to the finals.

It was during the last game that my big moment came. The game was tied with less than a minute to play. The other team was charging toward our goal.

I got into position. With all my might, I booted the ball to Sarah. She took off like a rocket and scored a goal.

As I said, I don't know how I let myself get talked into things. But I guess that sometimes it's a good thing.

Sarah has talked me into playing basketball this winter. And I've talked her into joining the History Club.

After all, together we can do just about anything. We're a team!

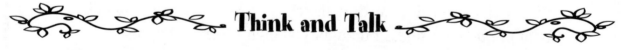

Think and Talk

What is fairness? Is the reaction that Rosie and Sarah have to each other at the beginning of the story fair? Explain.

Story Response

FAIRNESS

Directions

Answer the questions.

1. Why did Rosie not like Sarah at the beginning of the story?

_____

_____

2. How do the girls overcome their dislike of each other?

_____

_____

3. Why is a prejudiced person not fair?

_____

_____

4. What are two ways players show fairness in a soccer game?

_____

_____

_____

5. Tell about a disagreement you had with a friend. How did you solve the problem? Was the solution fair? Explain.

_____

_____

_____

A Fair Swing

FAIRNESS

A fair person takes turns and shares. A fair person treats everyone the same.

Directions

Look for ways your classmates are fair during class and on the playground. Write on a swing the name of the person and tell about the fair action. Then, hang the swing on the tree.

Name

Name

Name _____   Date _____

Fair or Foul?

A fair person is careful before making a decision. A fair person gets all the facts and considers what other people think when making a decision.

FAIRNESS

Directions

Suppose you are playing soccer with friends. You run and kick the ball before it rolls out of bounds. A player on the other team says you kicked the ball while it was foul. Write a paragraph to tell how to solve the problem fairly.

_____

_____

_____

_____

_____

_____

_____

_____

_____

_____

_____

_____

_____

_____

_____

_____

Fair Square

FAIRNESS

A fair person is open-minded and just. A fair person treats everyone the same.

Directions

Cut out the shape. Fold it to make a cube. Tape the sides together. Then, play Fair Square.

You blame Ann for taking your crayons before you ask questions.

You take the same number of cookies as your friends.

Everyone except Mike has a baseball hat. You laugh at Mike.

You tell Sue that she can be your friend, but only if she cleans out your desk.

Your friends say the new girl is mean. You say they should get to know her and not say bad things.

Jeff breaks your pencil. You ask if he can give you a new one to replace it.

How to Play Fair Square

1. Play with a partner. Take turns rolling the cube.

2. Decide if the action is fair or not fair. You get 1 point for each fair action. You do not get any score for an unfair action.

3. The first player with 10 points wins.

Trustworthiness

A trustworthy person is honest, reliable, and loyal. This means always telling the truth, even when it is difficult. A trustworthy person can be relied upon to fulfill his or her commitments. Trustworthiness also means being loyal to friends and family members. This last concept, loyalty, can be hard for students. Loyalty to friends may cause students to feel caught between friends and what is morally right. This is especially true in regard to keeping secrets. Stress to students the difference between good and harmful secrets. Lastly, explain to students that trust is built up over time and that once it is broken, it can be hard to rebuild.

The basic qualities of trustworthiness include:
- Support your family and friends.
- Tell the truth.
- Do what you say you will do.
- Be on time.
- Keep secrets that do not harm others.
- Do what is right, even if it is hard to do.

About the Symbol
The basic qualities of trustworthiness are easy for students to understand. However, practicing them can be more of a challenge. The tree itself is a symbol to stand straight, strong, and firm in words and actions. The group of trees represents being loyal to family members and friends.

About the Story (pages 22–24)
The Boy Who Cried Wolf by Aesop
A boy watching a flock of sheep plays tricks on the townspeople by crying "Wolf!" several times when there is no wolf. Each time the people come running to scare away the wolf. When the wolf finally does arrive, the people do not run to the boy's aid, thinking he is playing tricks again.

About the Activities
Activity 1: Tree-ific Trustworthiness
(page 25)
Review the qualities of trustworthiness with students. Then assign partners. Ask each partner to complete the activity page describing the ways his or her partner shows trustworthiness. Have students hang the trees on the theme bulletin board.

Activity 2: Time for Trustworthiness
(page 26)
Invite students to tell about the after-school activities they regularly participate in, including lessons, scouts, and sports. Then create a model of a time schedule that identifies the actions (dressing, finding equipment, eating a snack, travel time, etc.) and the clock time each takes in order to arrive on time.

Activity 3: A Trustworthy Helper (page 27)
Ask students to share how they feel when an adult or friend doesn't follow through on his or her promises. Then challenge students to use this activity to demonstrate that they can be counted on to help consistently.

Group Project
Divide students into six groups. Assign each group one of the qualities of trustworthiness listed above. Have them write a skit that reflects the quality. Provide simple props for the students to use when they present the skit.

At-home
Remind students that part of being trustworthy is to complete homework and to turn it in on time. Encourage students to keep a homework log to help them track assignments.

Related Reading
Harriet the Spy by Louise Fitzhugh
My Friend Flicka by Mary O'Hara
Tales of a Fourth Grade Nothing
    by Judy Blume

The Boy Who Cried Wolf

by Aesop

TRUSTWORTHINESS

Once there was a boy who looked after the sheep. He followed them as they grazed on the green grass up in the hills. One day he decided to play a trick on the people in the town.

So the boy shouted, "Wolf! Wolf!"

All the people ran up the hill. They shouted and clapped their hands very loudly to scare the wolf away.

"Where is the wolf?" they asked.

The boy just laughed at them. "There is no wolf," he said.

The people were angry when they found out that the boy had played a trick on them. They unhappily walked back down the hill.

Some days later, the boy decided to play the same trick again. He shouted very loudly, "Wolf! Wolf!"

The people ran up the hill again. They shouted and clapped their hands very loudly to scare the wolf away.

"Where is the wolf?" they asked.

The boy just laughed at them. "There is no wolf," he answered.

The people were very angry. The boy had played the same trick on them.

"Do not play any more tricks," they said. "Only shout when there IS a wolf!"

The people frowned as they walked back down the hill.

After a few more days, the boy decided to play his trick a third time. Again he cried, "Wolf! Wolf!"

Once more the people ran up the hill. They shouted and clapped their hands very loudly to scare the wolf away.

"Where is the wolf?" they asked.

The boy just laughed at them. "There is no wolf. I fooled you again," he said.

This time the people were very, very angry. They did not want to be fooled again. They grumbled as they stomped back down the hill.

Then one day a wolf looked out of the woods. The boy ran and hid behind a rock. He shouted, "Wolf! Wolf!"

But this time, no one came. The boy had tricked the people too many times.

"That silly boy is playing his tricks again," the people said. "He will not fool us. We will not run up the hill this time."

The wolf rushed out of the woods. The boy stayed behind the rock. He watched the wolf kill all the sheep. As soon as the wolf was gone, the boy ran down the hill as fast as he could.

When the boy got to the town, he told the people about the wolf and the sheep. "Why did you not come when I called? The wolf has killed all the sheep," he said.

"You told too many lies," said one man.

"Yes," agreed a woman. "When you tell that many lies, no one will believe you when you do tell the truth."

Think and Talk

What is trustworthiness? How did the boy in the story break the trust of the people who lived in the town?

Story Response

TRUSTWORTHINESS

Directions

Answer the questions.

1. What is the job of the boy in the story?

_____

_____

2. Why do the people not trust the boy at the end of the story?

_____

_____

3. What makes a person trustworthy?

_____

_____

4. Tell what it means when someone says, "Honor your word."

_____

_____

5. Are you trustworthy? Give one example that shows you are a trustworthy person.

_____

_____

_____

Name _____   Date _____

Tree-ific Trustworthiness

A trustworthy person is loyal. This means that the person is a good friend or family member. The person keeps secrets and stands by the people he or she cares about.

Directions

Work with a partner. Think about one way the partner is trustworthy. Write about it on the tree. Then, glue your tree and your partner's tree beside each other on another sheet of paper.

_____
Name

_____

_____

_____

_____

_____

_____

_____

Name _____   Date _____

Time for Trustworthiness

TRUSTWORTHINESS

A trustworthy person always arrives on time.

Directions

Complete the calendar. Write in the classes, lessons, or meetings you have each day. Then, write the time each happens.

Monday	Tuesday	Wednesday	Thursday	Friday

Directions

Choose one activity from the calendar. Make a time schedule listing what you need to do to get there on time. Be sure to include time to change clothes and travel to the activity.

_____

_____

_____

_____

_____

Name _____   Date _____

A Trustworthy Helper

Trustworthy people do what they say they will do.

Directions

What can you do for each person? Write it on a hand. Give it to each person.
Now do it!

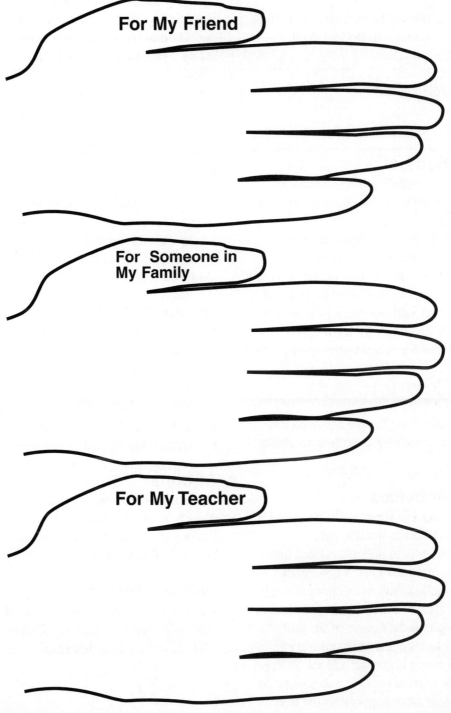

For My Friend

For Someone in
My Family

For My Teacher

Responsibility

Responsibility is the characteristic that is based on obligation. In a world full of choices, responsibility prompts individuals to be accountable for who they are and what they do. They have a moral duty to follow through and complete a task. It may mean that a person must impose self-restraint to succeed or to persevere if problems arise. Moreover, a responsible person is accountable for decisions—good or bad.

The basic qualities of responsibility include:
- Know what you are to do and do it.
- Think before you act.
- Do your best.
- Keep on trying.
- Be positive.
- Accept the consequences of your choices.

About the Symbol

For students, responsibility often means an obligation to complete a task, such as feeding the dog or picking up toys. At this age, they also need to think about consequences and perseverance. The symbols of the rake and leaves are clearly representative of the work and perseverance aspect, but it should be pointed out to students that without raking, there are consequences of an unsightly lawn and potential problems for harming the spring grass.

About the Poem (pages 29–31)

Mr. Nobody by Anonymous
Mr. Nobody is to blame for the mishaps in a house because no one else is willing to claim responsibility.

About the Activities

Activity 1: Raking Up Responsibility (page 32)
Review with students the qualities of responsibility. Help them understand that the word *job* means more than just a task or an assignment. Then, ask students to brainstorm how these qualities relate to the symbol of the leaves and rake. Throughout the course of the unit, remind students to recognize responsible classmates by writing about the actions on the leaves. You may wish to provide a special prize for students whose names appear on the tree.

Activity 2: Responsibility at Home (page 33)
Explain to students that consequences are the actions that happen after a choice has been made. For example, if a student watches television instead of doing homework, the consequence is that the child gets a poor grade. Then invite students to tell about jobs they have at home. You may wish to model how to substitute some of the jobs for the lines in the poem to make the assignment easier.

Activity 3: Puzzled About Responsibility (page 34)
Review all the qualities of a responsible person. Then encourage students to write a sentence about their favorite one.

Group Project

Invite students to make a Student Responsibility Handbook. Have them pretend that a visitor from another planet has arrived. They need to explain to the visitor the rules of how a responsible student should act. Make a list of students' suggestions. Let each student choose one to illustrate. Bind the pages to make a book.

At-home

Ask students to list on a calendar all of their weekly house chores and responsibilities. Encourage them to complete each one without being reminded of the task.

Related Reading

Anne of Green Gables by L. M. Montgomery
Henry Huggins by Beverly Cleary
Why Work? by Judi Jennings

Name _____   Date _____

Mr. Nobody

by Anonymous

RESPONSIBILITY

I know a funny little man,

As quiet as a mouse,

Who does the mischief that is done

In everybody's house!

There's no one ever sees his face,

And yet we all agree

That every plate we break was cracked

By Mr. Nobody.

'Tis he who always tears our books,

Who leaves the door ajar,

He pulls the buttons from our shirts,

And scatters pins afar;

That squeaking door will always squeak,

For, friend, don't you see,

We leave the oiling to be done

By Mr. Nobody.

He puts damp wood upon the fire,

So that kettles cannot boil;

His are the feet that bring in mud,

And all the carpets soil.

The papers always are mislaid,

Who had them last but he?

There's not one tosses them about

But Mr. Nobody.

The fingermarks upon the door

By none of us are made;

We never leave the blinds unclosed,

To let the curtains fade;

The ink we never spill; the boots

That lying 'round you see

Are not our boots; they all belong

To Mr. Nobody!

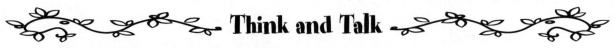

Think and Talk

What is responsibility? Why do the people in the poem blame
Mr. Nobody?

Name _____   Date _____

Poem Response

Directions

Answer the questions.

1. Who can see Mr. Nobody?

_____

_____

_____

2. Name two things Mr. Nobody gets blamed for in the poem.

_____

_____

3. What would a responsible person do if he or she walked across a carpet with muddy shoes?

_____

_____

4. Why do people not like to say they did something wrong?

_____

_____

_____

5. Does a Mr. Nobody visit your house? Explain.

_____

_____

_____

Name _____   Date _____

Raking Up Responsibility

RESPONSIBILITY

Responsible people know what jobs they are to do, and they do
their best to complete them. If responsible people face problems
while working, they keep trying until the job is done.

Directions

Look for ways your classmates show responsibility. Write the name of the
person on a leaf and tell how the person shows responsibility. Then, hang the
leaf on the tree.

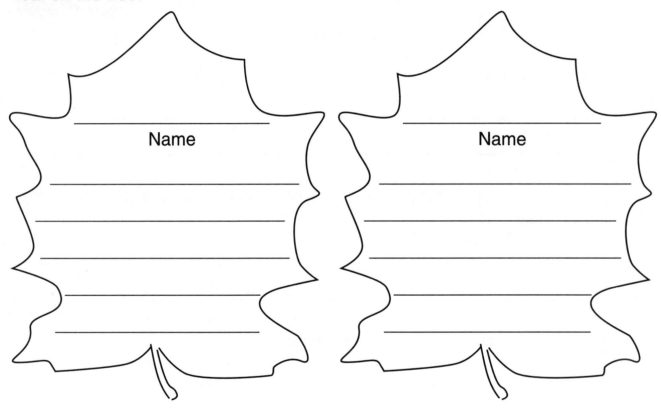

Name

Name

Directions

What can you do to be more responsible?

_____

_____

_____

Responsibility at Home

RESPONSIBILITY

What would happen if a job was not done? A responsible person thinks about how some choices may hurt other people and things.

Directions

What are some jobs that you have at home? Do you always complete them? Write another verse to the poem that tells about Mr. Nobody living in your house.

_____

_____

_____

_____

_____

_____

_____

Directions

What would happen if you did not do your jobs?

_____

_____

_____

_____

_____

Puzzled About Responsibility

RESPONSIBILITY

Responsibility means knowing what jobs need to be done and then doing them. The task may be hard or take a long time. But responsible people try to be cheerful and to do their best work.

Directions

Think of a sentence about responsibility. Write it on the plate. Cut out the plate. Then, cut the plate into pieces to make a puzzle. Trade puzzles with a classmate.

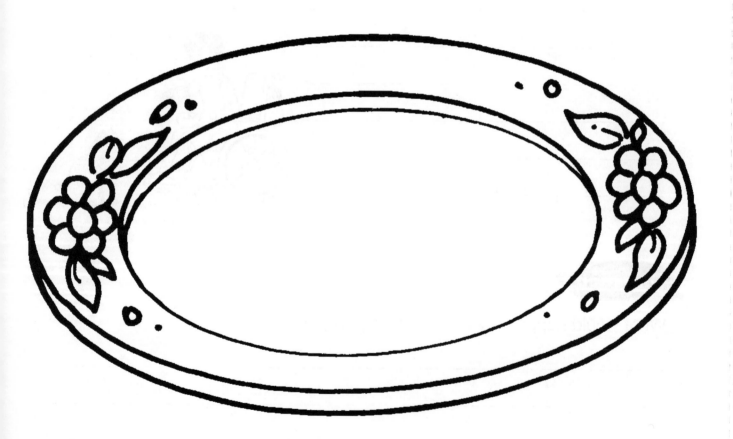

Respect

The way to show respect can vary from culture to culture, but this characteristic centers on treating each other and ourselves with consideration and dignity. The primary thought is to treat others as you want to be treated—the Golden Rule. This involves using good manners, practicing nonviolence, taking care of others' property, and respecting those who are different.

The basic qualities of respect include:
- Accept differences in others.
- Follow the Golden Rule.
- Respond to anger and insults peacefully.
- Use good manners.
- Be polite.

About the Symbol

Most students know of the Golden Rule—"Do unto others as you would have them do unto you." But at this age, students are beginning to form social groups based on interests and other identity factors. It is the ideal time for them to learn and practice tolerating those who are different. The different trees symbolize that there are many different trees in a forest, but their uniqueness is what makes the forest interesting and fun to visit.

About the Story (pages 36–39)
The Rerun by Barry Brook
Matt dropped the baton in a relay race the previous year. Samantha rudely reminds him of the fact. But the team, including Cliff and Susan, gets together again and practices. They win the race this time!

About the Activities

Activity 1: The Forest of Respect (page 40)
If possible, display pictures of different trees. Point out that there are many different trees in a forest. Discuss how much fun it is to walk in a forest and look at different trees. Then invite students to compare a forest to their classroom. Guide them to understand that many different people make up the classroom. Brainstorm with students why it is important to have different kinds of people and to accept their differences.

Activity 2: Some Words About Respect (page 41)
Remind students that using good manners is a sign of respect. Encourage students to talk about home and school manners. Remind students that Samantha in *The Rerun* did not have good manners because she called Matt names and made him feel bad for a mistake. Then, talk about the importance of good manners on the playground.

Activity 3: Respect the Golden Rule (page 42)
Discuss with students the meaning of the Golden Rule. Review examples of ways the characters in *The Rerun* did and did not exemplify the Golden Rule.

Group Project

Help students make life-size paper dolls by tracing their bodies on butcher paper. Allow them several days to draw features and clothing. Then give students paper to write a speech bubble telling how they are unique and different. Hang the paper dolls and bubbles in the hallway with this verse:
We're all different.
As you can see.
But we treat each other
RESPECTFULLY!

At-home

Ask students to find ways that family members show respect to each other.

Related Reading

The Hundred Dresses by Eleanor Estes
Mufaro's Beautiful Daughters: An African Tale by John Steptoe

The Rerun

by Barry Brook

RESPECT

Matt and Cliff walked home from school. It was Friday afternoon.

"Let's get our bikes and go to the comic book store," said Matt.

Cliff liked the idea. "I get my allowance today. We'll see if anything new came in."

The boys turned the corner onto Lake Street. They saw brightly colored signs on the telephone poles. They ran to the first pole. The signs were for the county fair.

"Remember how great the rides were?" asked Matt.

"The Ferris wheel was the best," answered Cliff.

"I liked the whip," Matt added.

"Remember the relay race?" asked Cliff.

Matt's smile seemed to vanish. "I remember we came in last. And it was my fault," said Matt. "I dropped the baton!"

"I didn't even think about that," said Cliff. "I just remember how much fun it was. Let's ask Samantha and Susan if they'll be on our team again."

Matt wasn't at all sure he wanted to be in another relay race. Matt couldn't forget what had happened last year. "We were leading," he said. "Samantha put the baton right in my hand...."

"And you dropped it," said Cliff. "It happens."

"I was so busy looking at the finish line that I didn't concentrate on the baton," Matt remembered.

"Then other runners came along. Someone kicked the baton. You couldn't even find it for a while," Cliff replied, grinning.

Matt didn't smile. "We came in last," he said.

"Matt, everyone makes mistakes. My dad says that's why they put erasers on pencils. So what do you think? Should we ask the girls?" asked Cliff.

"Okay," said Matt. He hoped the girls had forgotten his mistake. But he was afraid that Samantha would remember it and laugh at him.

"I like Samantha," said Matt. "But sometimes she is scary."

"What do you mean?" asked Cliff.

"Well, we both got an A in math," said Matt. "But my grade was a 95 and hers was a 98. She was so happy she beat me. That bothered me."

"Susan's not like that," said Cliff.

"I know," said Matt. "Okay, you ask Samantha. I'll ask Susan."

When the boys arrived at Susan's house, both girls were sitting on the front steps.

"Are you going to the fair next week?" asked Matt.

"Of course," Samantha answered. "Isn't everyone?"

Cliff looked at Matt. Then he asked slowly, "Do you want to be on the relay team with us again?"

The two girls looked at each other. "Only if Mr. Butterfingers puts glue all over his hand," Samantha said.

Matt knew he could depend on Samantha to say something like that. And, most likely, she had more to say.

"Come on, Sam, we had fun last year," said Susan.

"Oh sure," replied Samantha. "It's really fun to be on a last-place team. Maybe we'll get a loser's medal."

Matt couldn't take any more. "We're going to win this time!" he shouted.

"Oh really? How's that going to happen?" Samantha asked in a sharp voice.

"Because this time we're going to practice," Matt said. His voice was strong.

The other kids looked at each other. Then Cliff said, "No more jokes. No teasing. We're a team!"

The girls joined in. "You can depend on us. Let's start tomorrow!"

Matt was too excited to go to the comic book store now. "See you in the morning," he said.

The next day the team started early. They ran up and down the street. They passed the baton back and forth. When they dropped it, they tried again.

Samantha didn't tease. Matt didn't moan. Their team was good!

Saturday came. People crowded into the fair. There were dog and cat shows, farm animals, and lots of food. And, of course, there was the relay race.

As the runners were called to the starting line, Cliff shouted, "We're good!"

The team huddled together and joined hands.

"Ready, team?" yelled Susan.

"Ready to win!" shouted Matt, Samantha, and Cliff.

And they did!

Think and Talk

What is respect? Does Samantha show respect? Explain.

Story Response

RESPECT

Directions

Answer the questions.

1. Why did Samantha call Matt "Mr. Butterfingers"?

_____

_____

2. How does Matt feel about Samantha at the beginning of the story? At the end of the story? Explain.

_____

_____

3. People show respect by using good manners. What are some other ways people show respect?

_____

_____

4. If someone hurts you, how should you act in return?

_____

_____

5. What are some ways that you show respect in school?

_____

_____

_____

_____

_____

Name _____ Date _____

The Forest of Respect

One way to show respect is to accept all people, even if they are different.

Directions

Look for ways your classmates show respect. Write the name of the person on a tree and tell what he or she did. Then, tape the tree in the Forest of Respect.

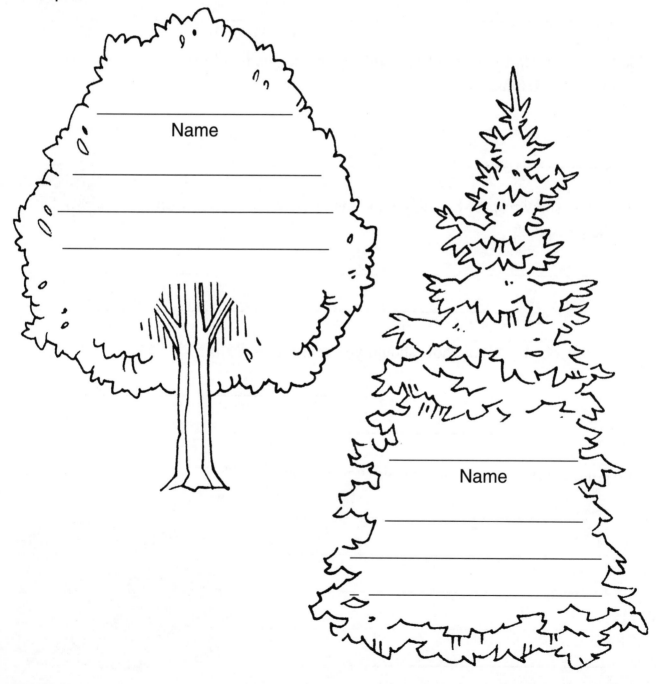

Name

Name

Some Words About Respect

One way to show respect is to use good manners. People who use good manners say and do nice things.

Directions

Look at the cartoon. Write sayings that show good manners on the playground.

Name _____   Date _____

Respect the Golden Rule

RESPECT

One way to show respect is to follow the Golden Rule. The Golden Rule says *Do unto others as you would have them do unto you.*

Directions

What does the Golden Rule mean? Write it in your own words. Then, draw a picture to go along with it.

_____

_____

_____

_____

Citizenship

We live in a democratic society where freedom and independence are prized and treasured. Citizens have a moral obligation to do their share to honor and improve on these traditions. Citizenship involves making a community better. It can be done by cooperating, obeying rules and laws, voting, and protecting the environment. Moreover, to make wise decisions for these activities, a citizen should learn about the issues.

The basic qualities of citizenship include:
- Work to make the community better.
- Follow laws and rules.
- Be a good neighbor.
- Cooperate.
- Keep the environment safe.
- Learn about activities in the community.
- Vote.

About the Symbol

The community is the focus of citizenship for students at this age. The community includes neighborhoods, businesses, schools, and nature areas. In recent years, society has increased its awareness of the environment, the interdependence between people and the land, and the impact people have on it. The bird is a symbol of nature, and the feeder represents the important role people have in taking care of it.

About the Story (pages 44–47)

The Greening of Harlem by Stephanie Hurley
A community works together to restore the parks to a place where people can safely play, grow flowers and food, and visit.

About the Activities

Activity 1: Fly High with Citizenship (page 48)
Lead students in a discussion of citizenship. Ask them how the birds are a symbol of this quality. Lead them to understand that citizenship involves caring for the environment. You may wish to provide a special treat for students whose names appear on the birds.

Activity 2: Words of Citizenship (page 49)
Briefly review the qualities of citizenship. Then discuss how those qualities appear in the story *The Greening of Harlem*. Tell students they will need to remember both the qualities and the story to complete the page.

Activity 3: You're a Citizen—Make Your Vote Count (page 50)
Explain to children that voting is a privilege that people living in a democratic society enjoy. Then ask students why it is important to learn about the people running for the positions, as well as why it is important to vote.

Group Project

Review how the community in *The Greening of Harlem* cooperated to improve the park. Then ask students to think about places around the school campus that need some care. Work with school officials to beautify the area.

At-home

Ask students to illustrate at least four rules they follow at home.

Related Reading

The Garden of Happiness by Erika Tamar
Grandfather's Dream by Holly Keller
The Great Kapok Tree by Lynne Cherry

The Greening of Harlem
by Stephanie Hurley

This story is based on the Greening of Harlem program.
It began in Harlem, a section of New York City, in 1989.

CITIZENSHIP

It was a hot day in the city. Keeba needed some fresh air.

"I'm going to ride bikes with Lee," Keeba told her mother.

The wind cooled her face as she rode past the park. Off to the side, she saw some older kids shouting and pushing each other. One boy kicked over a trash can. Keeba rode faster.

Lee was taking her bike outside when Keeba rode up.

"What's the hurry?" Lee asked.

"There was a fight in the park. It scared me," Keeba said. Keeba felt better with her friend.

The two girls rode to the park. There Keeba saw her neighbor, Monica. Monica was whispering to a friend and pointing at her. "That Monica is so mean!" she thought.

As Keeba turned to look at Monica, her tire hit a can. The handle bars jerked out of her hands. Keeba fell and hit her head. Keeba ended up in the hospital with her mother by her side.

"This is Dr. Barlow," her mother said.

"Hi, Keeba! You have a bad bump on your head," said Dr. Barlow. "What happened?"

"I ran over something at the park," said Keeba.

"I see many children who are hurt in the park. I'm meeting with a group of people to talk about making the park safer. Why don't you and your parents come to the meeting? Tell your neighbors, too!" said Dr. Barlow.

"We'll be there!" said Keeba's mother.

Keeba asked her friends to go to the meeting with their parents. Everyone knew someone who had been hurt at the park.

"I can't even sit in the park with my friends!" said an older man.

"Our children need a safe place to play!" Keeba's mother said.

At the meeting, the people wrote a petition. It said:

THE PARKS ARE THE PROPERTY OF THE CITY. PLEASE HELP US FIX THEM SO OUR CHILDREN CAN PLAY SAFELY.

The city agreed to help. It started a program to make the parks better. Planning began right away.

A woman from a playground company came to Keeba's school. She asked the children to draw pictures for her. She wanted the children's pictures to show what they would like on the playground.

Ms. Cozart from the Parks Department came to teach the children about plants. They grew tomato plants and flowers from seeds. They learned how to care for them.

The day came for the work to begin. A huge crane picked up the broken seesaws, swings, and jungle gyms in the park. It dropped them into dump trucks. Many truckloads of trash left the park that day. Keeba saw Monica standing by and watching the work, too.

Next, the work began on the playground. First, the adults talked with the older kids. They taught them how to be group leaders.

Monica became the leader of Keeba's group. "Good work, kids!" she said.

Keeba nudged Lee. "Maybe Monica's not so bad after all," she said.

The adults put metal poles in the ground. They hung ladders and slides to them. Neighbors made chicken, beans, rice, and salad for everyone. In two days the playground was done!

Big kids pushed little kids on the new swings.

The next day trucks dumped piles of dirt in the park. Keeba and Lee planted corn, beans, flowers, and the baby tomato plants from school. A group of older kids came to water the plants. Keeba saw Monica carrying a watering can.

Finally, the kids painted a giant mural at the new park. Keeba reached high over her head to paint. Lee held the can. Monica held the ladder. It was a real team effort!

That summer, the park was filled with children and their families. Keeba loved seeing the flowers and vegetables grow. She helped Monica water and weed the garden.

By fall, many of the vegetables were ripe. Keeba asked her teacher, "When can we eat our vegetables?"

"Let's have a feast to celebrate our new park and garden," Lee suggested.

The cooks at the school helped Keeba's class make the feast. They used vegetables they had grown in the garden.

The children invited everyone who helped fix up the park. They danced, played, and enjoyed the fresh food from their own garden!

The next afternoon, Keeba and Lee went to the park for the Bicycle Safety Program. Monica walked by. She was on her way to a baseball game.

"Good luck!" the girls called to her.

"Thanks!" she replied. "I think we're on a winning streak!"

"We sure are!" said Keeba. She put on her helmet. "In more ways than one!"

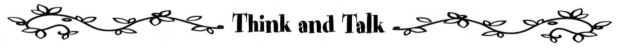

Think and Talk

What is citizenship? What did the people living in Harlem do to make their community better?

Name _____   Date _____

Story Response

CITIZENSHIP

Directions

Answer the questions.

1. Why was the park unsafe?

_____

_____

2. How did the people in the story change? Why do you think they changed?

_____

_____

3. Why is it important for a citizen to follow laws and rules?

_____

_____

_____

_____

4. What are some things good neighbors do for each other?

_____

_____

_____

5. Tell how you cooperate in school.

_____

_____

_____

Name _____   Date _____

Fly High with Citizenship

Good citizens cooperate to get a job done. They work together as a team.

Directions

Look for ways your classmates cooperate. Write their names on the birds and tell how they cooperated. Then, put the birds on the tree.

_____

Name

_____

_____

Name

_____

Name _____ Date _____

Words of Citizenship

A good citizen works to make the community a better place for everyone to live.

Directions

Complete each sentence. Then, use the numbered letters to answer the question, "What award will you win when your behavior is shipshape?"

1. A good __ __ __ __ __ __ __ works to improve the community.
          1   2

2. A __ __ __ __ __ __ __ __ is someone who lives next to you.
   3

3. Adults __ __ __ __ for a President every four years.
       4

4. People on a __ __ __ __ cooperate to get a job done.
      5

5. A citizen follows laws and __ __ __ __ __ .
             6

6. Children go to __ __ __ __ __ __ to learn.
      7 8

7. A __ __ __ __ is a place to swing, slide, and play.
   9

__ __ __ __ __ __ __ __ __ __
7 1 4 1 2 5 3 6 8 1 9

You're a Citizen—Make Your Vote Count

CITIZENSHIP

People vote to choose who will make the rules in a community. It is important for citizens to learn who those people are and what ideas they have to improve the community.

Directions

Two students want to help the principal at school. All the children get to vote for the one they think will be better. Read about each student.

Ben gets to school early every day. He helps the librarian. Ben puts books on shelves and finds special books that teachers want. He even helps students look for facts on the computer. Once a week, he goes to read books to a first-grade class. Ben wants to raise money to buy more books for the library.

Jan likes to play basketball. During outside free time, she forms teams to play a basketball game. She makes sure everyone gets to play. When some of the students get angry, Jan helps them solve the problem. She wants to find a way for students to stay after school to play if they want to.

Directions

Whom would you vote for? Explain.

_____

_____

_____

_____

_____

Wrapping Up

Some of the character traits, like caring, are easy for students to understand, identify, and practice. Some of the character traits, such as trustworthiness, are more intrinsic, and therefore, harder for students to conceptualize. Learning about each individual character trait is important. But in reality, many of the character traits overlap. When there is caring, there is usually respect. When there is responsibility, there is often trustworthiness. The final unit develops the concept that many of the character traits intertwine and are important to live a healthy, moral life.

About the Story (pages 52–54)

No Problem by Betsy Franco
When the mother leaves for a job in another city, a family must learn to work together to cook, clean, and get ready for school.

About the Activities

Activity 1: A Story Showing Good Character (page 55)

Review all six character traits and the qualities associated with each. Encourage students to share examples of each.

Activity 2: Searching for Character (page 56)

Have students read the words and identify those that name character traits. Brainstorm how the other words relate to good character. Remind students that the puzzle words can be across, down, and diagonal.

Activity 3: A Picture of Good Character (page 57)

Review how the characters in *No Problem* exemplify caring, responsibility, etc. Then, display a picture that shows people exhibiting one of the traits. Have children name it. Next, provide a variety of magazines or pictures. Have students select one to cut out and glue to paper.

Activity 4: Questions About Character (page 58)

Now that students have completed all the units, have them choose two of the targeted character traits and then interview a person who exemplifies these traits.

Activity 5: Showing Good Character (page 59)

Students should have completed several of these forms throughout the course of the character education program. Have students select their best work and collect them in a decorated folder. The cover of the folder may be decorated with drawings or magazine pictures that show people demonstrating respect, citizenship, caring, or other positive character traits.

Activity 6: Character Calendar (page 60)

You may wish to plan a final group project in which the whole class selects a character trait to work on each day. The students then use the character calendar to record the trait chosen and how they exhibited the trait throughout the day.

Group Project

Help students plan a celebration of good character. Have them display their group projects from the previous units. For those completed outside the classroom, ask volunteers to draw pictures or write about the activities.

At-home

Ask students to tell family members about the story *No Problem*. Have them make a list telling how their family shows good character.

Related Reading

The Secret Garden by Frances Hodgson Burnett
Misty of Chincoteague by Marguerite Henry

No Problem

by Betsy Franco

Mom got a new job. She had to travel all the way to New York. She would be gone for ten days.

"We'll miss you, honey, but we'll be fine," Dad said.

We *were* fine the first day. We made our lunches in the morning. We loaded our dirty clothes in the washing machine. Then we left for school. Karen was a little late. But we got there.

We got take-out food for dinner. Homework was no problem. Dad is really good at helping us.

That night, the trouble started. We took our clothes out of the washing machine.

"My running socks are pink," Dad said.

"So is my white football shirt," I added.

I pulled Karen's new red socks out of the wet pile. Everyone groaned.

"Don't blame Karen," Dad said. "We all make mistakes."

There was also a problem at the dinner table. After three nights of take-out food, we started getting tired of it. Table manners had gone out the window. Sara rolled her eyes. She ate quickly. Then she would hurry off to do her homework.

Dad tried his best. But Mom seemed to help everyone follow the rules.

Another problem was getting up in the morning. Dad's an artist. He paints late at night. He set his alarm so he could help us get up. But he kept sleeping through it. We were late for school.

Then there were the lunches. We each made our own. Karen packed mostly snacks—chips, cookies, and something to drink.

By day five, we were anxious for Mom to come home.

"Dad," I said, "Five days is a long time. We've got to do something."

"You're right," Dad said. "Let's start with the clothes."

I'd seen a commercial on TV about soap that makes clothes white. We tossed all our pink clothes in a bucket of water and poured in the soap. Then we made piles for dark, light, and white clothes.

From then on, when something would go wrong, I would say, "No problem," and it seemed to help.

Next, we had to do something about dinner. I made a list of the meals we knew how to cook. Pretty soon, we had planned meals for the next five days. Things were looking up.

As for table manners, we started a list: Take turns setting the table. Clean up spills. Say *please* and *thank you*.

Getting up in the morning became "no problem" too. I set two alarms. One was way across the room. That way I had to get up to turn it off.

Dad was always up in time to help with the lunches. We stood in a line to make peanut butter and jelly sandwiches. Everybody had a job.

"No problem," we said to each other.

The day Mom got home, she thought she was in the wrong house. Dinner was on the table.

"I'm really surprised!" she said. "I didn't know you'd do so well. Now it's not so hard to tell you that I'll need to go to New York again."

We all began to laugh. We knew we'd be okay.

"No problem!" we all said at once.

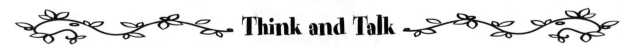

Think and Talk

How did the family show good character?

Name _____   Date _____

Story Response

WRAPPING UP

Directions

Answer the questions.

1. What were some problems the family had when the mother went to New York?

_____

_____

2. How did the family solve the problems?

_____

_____

3. How did the family show caring?

_____

_____

4. How did the family show responsibility?

_____

_____

5. How does your family show good character traits at home?

_____

_____

_____

Name _____ Date _____

A Story Showing Good Character

Directions

Name the character trait shown by the picture. Then, tell how the family in *No Problem* shows each.

 1. _____
_____

_____
_____
_____

 2. _____
_____

_____
_____
_____

 3. _____
_____

_____
_____
_____

 4. _____
_____

_____
_____
_____

 5. _____
_____

_____
_____
_____

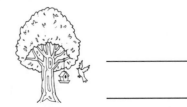 6. _____
_____

_____
_____
_____

Name _____   Date _____

Searching for Character

WRAPPING UP

Directions

Find words about character. The words are across, down, and diagonal. Circle them.

caring citizenship fairness help manners polite	
share rules responsibility truth trustworthiness respect	

```
Z A R T R U S T W O R T H I N E S S S
D I F F R E S P O N S I B I L I T Y H
W I C S A L S A W L M F A I K O P U A
A T U P S D G P L A B A P J L R E Q R
C R T O W S V H E L P I N M V T I T E
T U Z L A A R N I C A R I N G F O U G
I T A I D R T U P L T N W S E P O L E
Y H V T G R E M L K A E A S R R I K L
A S E E C I T I Z E N S H I P T S R E
H A P P I N Y Z Q T S S C L A U J M D
```

Name _____   Date _____

A Picture of Good Character

WRAPPING UP

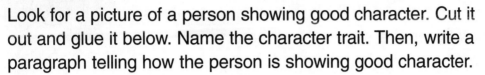
Directions

Look for a picture of a person showing good character. Cut it out and glue it below. Name the character trait. Then, write a paragraph telling how the person is showing good character.

_____

_____

_____

_____

_____

Name _____   Date _____

Questions About Character

Think of someone you admire. Ask that person the questions
below to find out how he or she shows the character trait
your teacher names.

Character Trait: _____

1. What does this character trait mean to you?

_____

_____

_____

2. How have you shown this character trait to others?

_____

_____

_____

_____

3. When has someone shown this character trait to you?

_____

_____

_____

_____

Name _____   Date _____

Showing Good Character

 **Directions**

Complete the paragraphs to tell how you showed good character.

On _____ , I showed the character trait of

_____.

Here is what I did:

_____

_____

_____.

It made me feel _____

because _____

_____

_____.

Next time I would _____

_____

_____

_____

_____

_____

_____

_____

_____.

Name _____   Date _____

Character Calendar

Month: _____   Dates: _____

_____

Monday   _____

_____

_____

Tuesday   _____

_____

_____

Wednesday   _____

_____

_____

Thursday   _____

_____

_____

Friday   _____

_____

_____

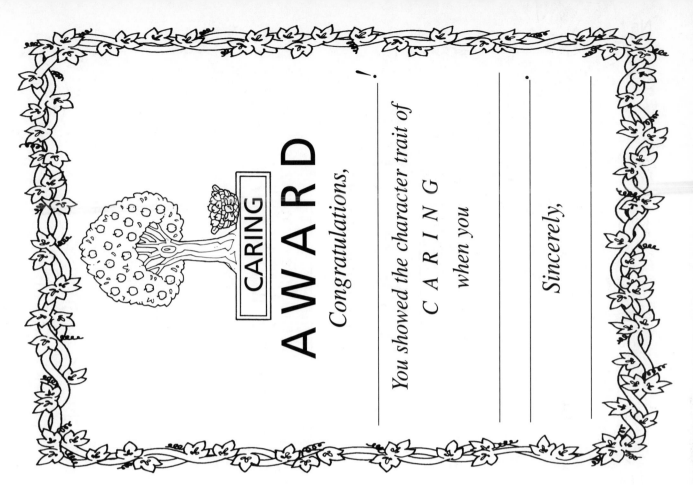

CARING AWARD

Congratulations,

You showed the character trait of C A R I N G when you

Sincerely,

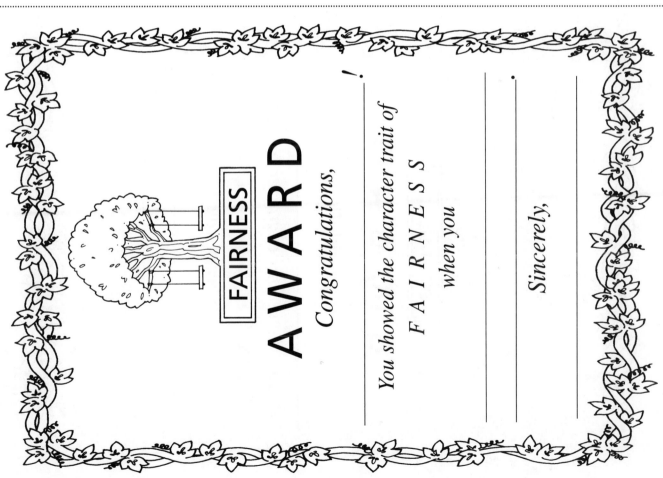

FAIRNESS AWARD

Congratulations,

You showed the character trait of F A I R N E S S when you

Sincerely,

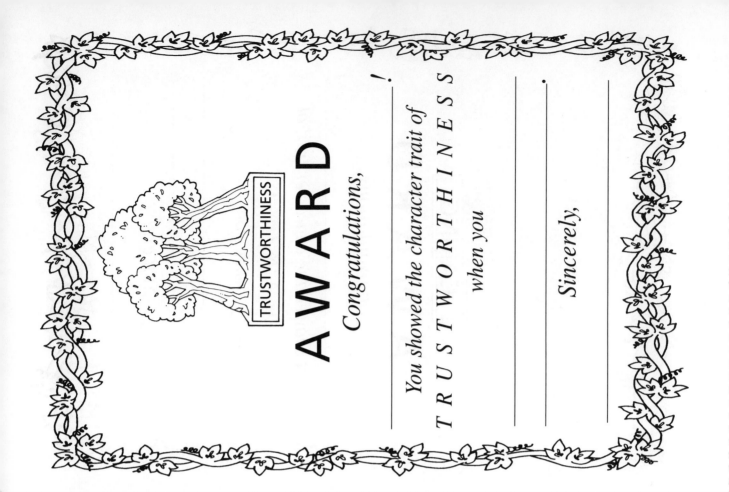

AWARD

TRUSTWORTHINESS

Congratulations,

You showed the character trait of
T R U S T W O R T H I N E S S
when you

Sincerely,

AWARD

RESPONSIBILITY

Congratulations,

You showed the character trait of
R E S P O N S I B I L I T Y
when you

Sincerely,

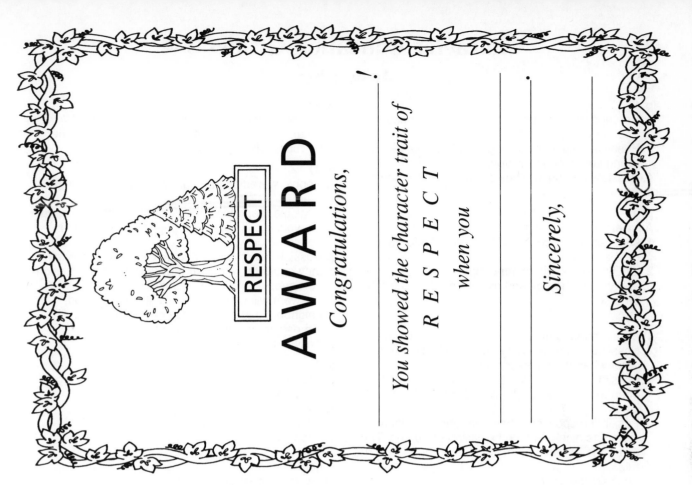

RESPECT

AWARD

Congratulations,

You showed the character trait of

R E S P E C T

when you

Sincerely,

CITIZENSHIP

AWARD

Congratulations,

You showed the character trait of

C I T I Z E N S H I P

when you

Sincerely,

Character Education Grades 3–4
Answer Key

p. 9
1. Serungal tells the boy to stop throwing rocks.
2. The ants collect the basket of scattered rice.
3. Possible responses: taking food to a sick person; telling someone thank you.
4. Possible response: They say or write "I'm sorry."
5. Answers will vary.

p. 12
Answers may vary slightly.
1. sad; help him get up and hold the bike for him to get back on
2. lonely; ask the girl to jump rope
3. angry; help the boy and girl find a solution for the argument

p. 17
1. Sarah laughed at her when she missed the ball.
2. Possible response: They began to know each other when they worked together.
3. Possible response: A prejudiced person is not open-minded. He or she will not think about new ideas.
4. Possible responses: They treat opposing team members nicely—no name calling or hurting. They share the ball with team members. They follow the rules.
5. Answers will vary.

p. 24
1. He takes care of the sheep.
2. He plays tricks on and lies to the people in the town.
3. Possible responses: They tell the truth.; They arrive on time.; They keep secrets.
4. It means you should keep a promise.
5. Answers will vary.

p. 31
1. No one can see Mr. Nobody because he is not real.
2. Possible responses: He breaks plates, leaves doors open, pulls buttons off shirts, leaves muddy footprints.
3. Possible responses: The person would clean it up or tell someone about the mess.
4. Possible response: People do not want to get in trouble.
5. Answers will vary.

p. 39
1. Matt dropped the baton in a relay race the year before.
2. He doesn't like Samantha because she makes fun of him at the beginning of the story. He likes her at the end because she stops making fun of him.
3. Possible responses: They don't hurt others.; They accept people as they are.
4. Answers will vary but should show that the students respond positively.
5. Answers will vary.

p. 41
Possible responses: That was a good throw.; Wow! You can jump so many times without stopping the jump rope.; May I please play?

p. 47
1. People were fighting, and there was trash on the ground.
2. Possible responses: Monica started being nice to the young children.; She began to take pride in her community.
3. Possible response: If people did not follow rules, they could do whatever they wanted to do. It might hurt people in the community.
4. Answers will vary but should show that good neighbors say kind words or do kind actions for the people who live close to them.
5. Answers will vary.

p. 49
1. citizen
2. neighbor
3. vote
4. team
5. rules
6. school
7. park
Answer: citizenship

p. 54
1. Possible responses: They washed red socks with white clothes.; The children were late for school.
2. Possible responses: They sorted clothes by colors; They set two alarm clocks.
3. Possible response: They helped each other fix lunches.
4. They set several alarm clocks so they could wake up and get to school in time.
5. Answers will vary.

p. 55
Accept reasonable explanations.
1. caring
2. fairness
3. trustworthiness
4. responsibility
5. respect
6. citizenship

p. 56

```
Z A R T R U S T W O R T H I N E S S S
D I F F R E S P O N S I B I L I T Y H
W I C S A L S A W L M F A I K O P U A
A T U P S D G P L A B A P J L R E Q R
C R T O W S V H E L P I N M V T I T E
T U Z L A A R N I C A R I N G F O U G
I T A I D R T U P L T N W S E P O L E
Y H V T G R E M L K A E A S R R I K L
A S E E C I T I Z E N S H I P T S R E
H A P P I N Y Z Q T S S C L A U J M D
```

CARING

CARING

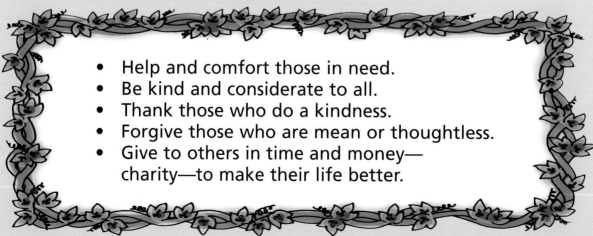

- Help and comfort those in need.
- Be kind and considerate to all.
- Thank those who do a kindness.
- Forgive those who are mean or thoughtless.
- Give to others in time and money—charity—to make their life better.

FAIRNESS

FAIRNESS

- Take turns and share.
- Treat people equally.
- Be open-minded and listen.
- Do not blame people carelessly.
- Do not take advantage of people.
- Let consequences fit the wrongful act.

TRUSTWORTHINESS

TRUSTWORTHINESS

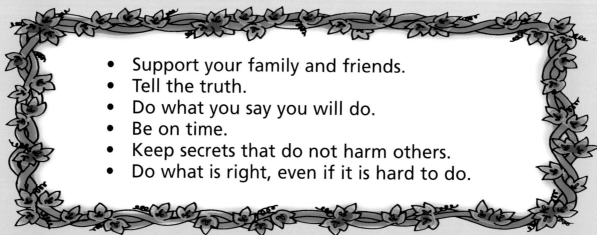

- Support your family and friends.
- Tell the truth.
- Do what you say you will do.
- Be on time.
- Keep secrets that do not harm others.
- Do what is right, even if it is hard to do.

RESPONSIBILITY

RESPONSIBILITY

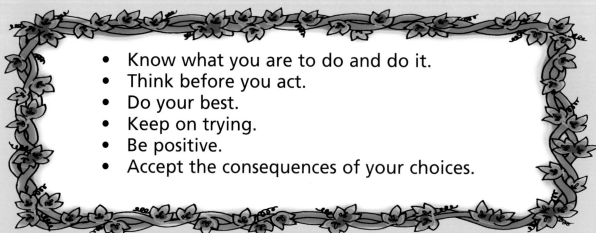

- Know what you are to do and do it.
- Think before you act.
- Do your best.
- Keep on trying.
- Be positive.
- Accept the consequences of your choices.

RESPECT

RESPECT

- Accept differences in others.
- Follow the Golden Rule.
- Respond to anger and insults peacefully.
- Use good manners.
- Be polite.

CITIZENSHIP

CITIZENSHIP

- Work to make the community better.
- Follow laws and rules.
- Be a good neighbor.
- Cooperate.
- Keep the environment safe.
- Learn about activities in the community.
- Vote.

DOMINOES

CITIZENSHIP	RESPECT	RESPONSIBILITY	TRUSTWORTHINESS	FAIRNESS	CARING

CITIZENSHIP	RESPECT	RESPONSIBILITY	TRUSTWORTHINESS	FAIRNESS	CARING

CITIZENSHIP	RESPECT	RESPONSIBILITY	TRUSTWORTHINESS	FAIRNESS	CARING

DOMINOES

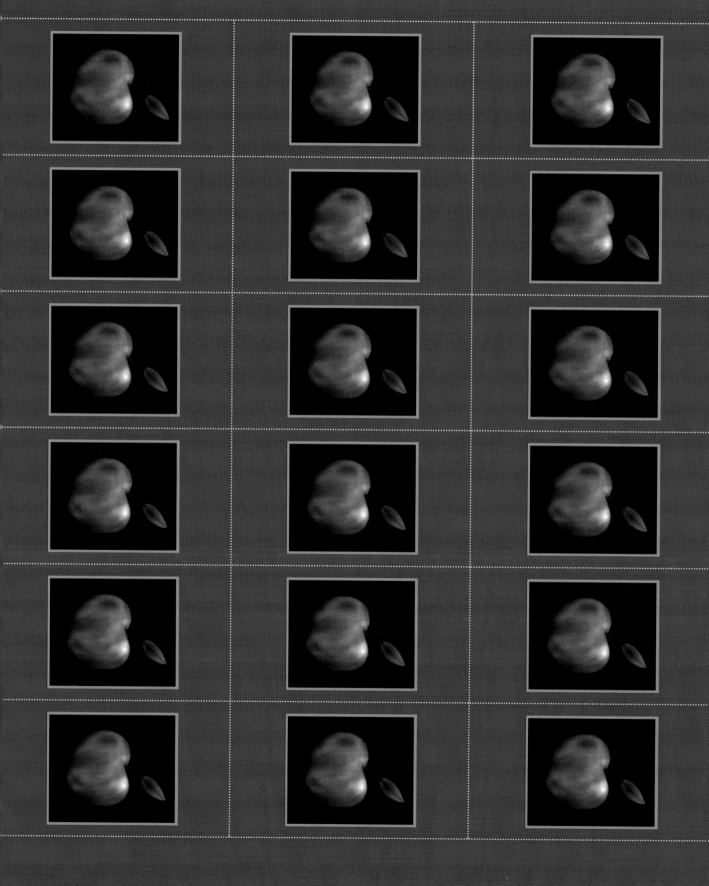

DOMINOES

CITIZENSHIP		CITIZENSHIP		CITIZENSHIP	
RESPECT		RESPECT		RESPECT	
RESPONSIBILITY		RESPONSIBILITY		RESPONSIBILITY	
TRUSTWORTHINESS		TRUSTWORTHINESS		TRUSTWORTHINESS	
FAIRNESS		FAIRNESS		FAIRNESS	
CARING		CARING		CARING	

DOMINOES

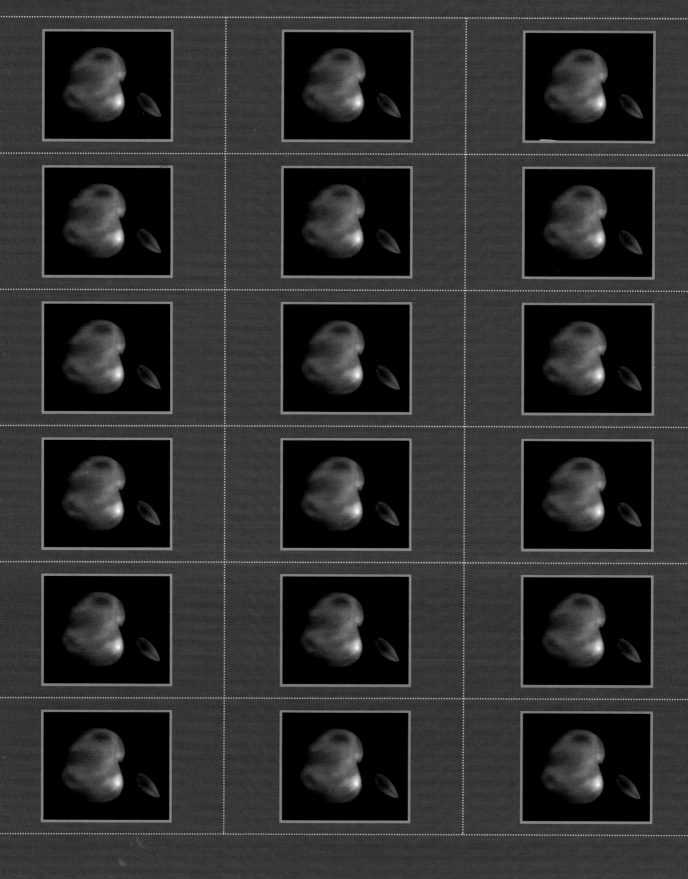